TOFU
The Ultimate Tofu Recipe Book

Les Ilagan

Table of Contents

INTRODUCTION

Tofu or soybean curd is a staple food in Asia and now it is being enjoyed worldwide. It is made of soybeans and is considered an excellent meat substitute because of its high nutrient profile, particularly its protein and micronutrient content.

The people from China have been eating tofu since ancient times, which introduced us to the different ways on how to prepare them. Truly, tofu is a versatile ingredient that offers many health benefits; that is why it is favored by many people, especially those who do not eat meat like the vegetarians or vegans.

This recipe book will help you create wonderful dishes that you and your loved ones will surely enjoy. You can prepare tofu as a main course, soup, salad, appetizer, or even as a dessert!

This book is a part of many cookbook series that I am writing, and I hope you have fun trying all the recipes here.

So, let's get started!

TOFU RECIPES

*Easy and Delicious Tofu Recipes
for Your Everyday Meals*

TRADITIONAL MA PO TOFU

Preparation Time	Total Time	Yield
10 minutes	25 minutes	4 servings

INGREDIENTS

- 1 tablespoon (7 g) cornstarch
- 2 tablespoons (30 ml) cold water
- 1 tablespoon (15 ml) peanut oil
- 1 tablespoon (10 g) garlic, minced
- 1 tablespoon (10 g) fresh ginger root, grated
- 1 (16 oz. or 450 g) package silken tofu, cut into 1-inch pieces
- 1/2 cup (125 ml) vegetable stock, unsalted
- 1/4 cup (60 ml) soy sauce
- 2 tablespoons (30 g) hot bean sauce
- 1 teaspoon (5 g) brown sugar
- 1/4 cup (15 g) green onions, chopped
- 1 teaspoon (5 ml) sesame oil

METHOD

- Mix together the cornstarch and water in a small bowl. Set aside.
- Heat the peanut oil in a large skillet over medium-high flame. Stir-fry garlic and ginger root until fragrant, about 1-2 minutes.
- Add the tofu, vegetable stock, soy sauce, hot bean sauce, and brown sugar. Cook, stirring gently for 5 minutes.

- Stir in cornstarch and water mixture. Cook, stirring until thickened, about 2-3 minutes. Remove from the heat and then stir in 1 teaspoon sesame oil.
- Transfer to a serving dish and sprinkle with green onions.
- Serve and enjoy.

NUTRITIONAL INFORMATION

Energy	Fat	Carbohydrates	Protein	Sodium
141 calories	7.8 g	8.9 g	9.2 g	671 mg

TOFU WITH SRIRACHA SAUCE

Preparation Time	Total Time	Yield
10 minutes	25 minutes	4 servings

INGREDIENTS

- 1 (16 oz. or 450 g) package extra-firm tofu
- 3 tablespoons (45 ml) vegetable oil
- 2 shallots (about 40 g each), chopped
- 1 teaspoon (3 g) garlic, minced
- 1 medium (125 g) red bell pepper, diced
- 1 medium (125 g) green bell pepper, diced
- 2 tablespoons (30 g) Sriracha sauce
- 1/4 cup spring (15 g) onion, chopped
- Salt and freshly ground black pepper

METHOD

- Cut the tofu into 1-inch slices.
- Heat 2 tablespoons of oil in a non-stick fry pan or skillet over medium-high flame. Cook the tofu until golden brown. Transfer to a clean plate and cut into 1-inch cubes. Set aside.
- Using the same pan, heat the remaining 1 tablespoon of oil. Sauté the chopped shallots and garlic for about 2-3 minutes.
- Add the bell peppers and Sriracha sauce; cook, stirring for 5 minutes.
- Add the tofu and spring onion; cook for another 2-3 minutes. Season to taste.

- Transfer to a serving dish.
- Serve and enjoy.

NUTRITIONAL INFORMATION

Energy	Fat	Carbohydrates	Protein	Sodium
200 calories	15.1 g	9.2 g	10.2 g	289 mg

TOFU SKEWERS WITH SESAME AND SPICY PEANUT SAUCE

Preparation Time	Total Time	Yield
10 minutes	25 minutes	6 servings

INGREDIENTS

- 1/4 cup (60 ml) vegetable oil
- 2 (16 oz. or 450 g) package extra-firm tofu
- 2 tablespoons (20 g) sesame seeds, toasted
- 12 decorative wooden skewers

Spicy Peanut Sauce:

- 1/4 cup (60 g) peanut butter
- 2 tablespoons (30 ml) soy sauce
- 2 tablespoons (30 ml) water
- 1 tablespoon (15 ml) lime juice
- 1 teaspoon (5 g) chili-garlic sauce
- 1 teaspoon (5 g) brown sugar
- 1 teaspoon (5 g) fresh ginger, grated

METHOD

- Mix together the peanut butter, soy sauce, water, lime juice, chili-garlic sauce, brown sugar, and ginger in a small bowl.
- Cut tofu into 1-inch slices.
- Heat the vegetable oil in a non-stick pan or skillet over medium-high flame. Fry the tofu slices until golden brown on both sides. Transfer to a chopping board

and cut into 1-inch cubes.

- Thread the tofu onto the skewers. Place in a serving dish.
- Drizzle with peanut sauce and sprinkle with toasted sesame seeds.
- Serve and enjoy.

NUTRITIONAL INFORMATION

Energy	Fat	Carbohydrates	Protein	Sodium
231 calories	17.7 g	6.5 g	15.9 g	369 mg

EASY TOFU SATAY

Preparation Time	Total Time	Yield
10 minutes	1 hour 30 minutes	12 servings

INGREDIENTS

- 2 (16 oz. or 450 g) package extra-firm tofu
- 12 wooden skewers

Marinade:

- 2/3 cup (165 ml) coconut milk
- 2 cloves (6 g) garlic, minced
- 1 tablespoon (15 g) brown sugar
- 1 teaspoon (2 g) curry powder
- Salt and freshly ground black pepper

Spicy Satay Sauce:

- 1 cup (250 ml) coconut milk
- 2 teaspoons (4 g) curry powder
- 2/3 cup (165 g) chunky peanut butter
- 1 cup (250 ml) chicken stock
- 1/4 cup (60 g) brown sugar
- 3 tablespoons (45 ml) lime juice
- 1 tablespoon (15 ml) soy sauce
- 1 teaspoon (5 g) chili paste
- Salt and freshly ground black pepper

METHOD

- Mix together the coconut milk, garlic, brown sugar, and curry powder. Season with salt and pepper. Stir until the sugar has dissolved. Transfer the marinade into a non-reactive container. Then, add the tofu; cover and marinate for 1 hour.
- Preheat your griddle or grill to medium-high.
- Thread your marinated tofu onto each wooden

skewer. Grill for about 5 minutes on each side or until browned and grill marks form.

- To make the Spicy Satay Sauce, combine the coconut milk, curry powder, peanut butter, chicken stock, brown sugar, and chili paste in a saucepan. Cook over medium flame for 10-12 minutes, stirring frequently until thickened. Remove from heat. Add in the lime juice and soy sauce. Stir and season to taste.
- Serve the tofu skewers in a serving platter with satay sauce on the side.
- Enjoy.

NUTRITIONAL INFORMATION

Energy	Fat	Carbohydrates	Protein	Sodium
199 calories	14.0 g	11.8 g	10.3 g	189 mg

TOFU VEGGIE KEBABS

Preparation Time	Total Time	Yield
10 minutes	50 minutes	8 servings

INGREDIENTS

- 1/2 cup (125 ml) olive oil
- 1/4 cup (60 ml) lime juice
- 1/4 teaspoon (0.5 g) dried thyme
- 1 (16 oz. or 450 g) package extra-firm tofu, cut into small cubes
- 1 small head broccoli, cut into florets
- 2 medium white onion (about 120 g each), quartered
- 2 medium bell pepper (about 125 g each), cut into 1-inch pieces
- 8 long wooden skewers
- Salt and freshly ground black pepper

METHOD

- Combine the oil, lime juice, and thyme in a large bowl.
- Add the tofu, broccoli, onion, and bell pepper. Toss to coat with marinade and then season with salt and pepper. Cover and let sit for 30 minutes to absorb flavors.
- Preheat your grill or griddle to high.
- Thread the marinated tofu and vegetables alternately onto the wooden skewers.
- Grill the tofu-veggie skewers for about 7 minutes on each side or until grill marks form, brushing with marinade occasionally.
- Transfer to a serving dish.

- Serve and enjoy.

NUTRITIONAL INFORMATION

Energy	Fat	Carbohydrates	Protein	Sodium
128 calories	8.9 g	8.7 g	6.3 g	121 mg

TOFU WITH RED CURRY AND MIXED VEGETABLES

Preparation Time	Total Time	Yield
10 minutes	40 minutes	6 servings

INGREDIENTS

- 2 tablespoons (30 g) butter
- 1 large white onion (about 150 g), thinly sliced
- 2 cloves (6 g) garlic, minced
- 2 tablespoons (12 g) red curry powder
- 1/2 teaspoon (1 g) cayenne pepper
- 1/2 teaspoon (1 g) coriander seed, ground
- 2 cups (300 g) broccoli florets, cut into small pieces
- 1 medium (60 g) carrot, cut into small pieces
- 1 medium (125 g) bell pepper, cut into strips
- 2 cups (500 ml) chicken stock
- 1 cup (250 g) heavy cream
- 1 cup (250 ml) milk
- 1 (16 oz. or 450g) package firm tofu, cut into small cubes
- Salt and freshly ground black pepper

METHOD

- Heat oil in a medium saucepan over medium-high flame. Stir-fry onion and garlic for about 3 minutes.
- Add the curry powder, cayenne pepper, and coriander. Cook for 1 minute, stirring constantly.
- Add the broccoli, carrot, bell pepper, and chicken

stock. Bring to a boil. Lower the heat and simmer for about 6-7 minutes.

- Stir in the cream, milk, and tofu. Cook for another 5 minutes, stirring frequently but gently. Season to taste.
- Transfer to a serving dish.
- Serve and enjoy.

NUTRITIONAL INFORMATION

Energy	Fat	Carbohydrates	Protein	Sodium
215 calories	15.7 g	12.3 g	9.7 g	280 mg

PAN-FRIED HOISIN TOFU WITH SESAME

Preparation Time	Total Time	Yield
5 minutes	15 minutes	4 servings

INGREDIENTS

- 1 (16 oz. or 450 g) package firm tofu
- 2 tablespoons (30 g) hoisin sauce
- 2 tablespoons (30 ml) peanut oil
- 1/4 cup (15 g) scallions, chopped
- 1 tablespoon (10 g) toasted sesame seeds
- Salt and freshly ground black pepper

METHOD

- Cut the tofu to make ¼-inch slices and brush each with hoisin sauce. Season with salt and pepper.
- Heat peanut oil in a non-stick fry pan over medium-high flame. Cook the seasoned tofu slices until golden brown on both sides.
- Transfer to a serving dish. Sprinkle with scallions and sesame seeds.
- Serve and enjoy.

NUTRITIONAL INFORMATION

Energy	Fat	Carbohydrates	Protein	Sodium
171 calories	12.8 g	6.4 g	10.0 g	291 mg

TOFU AND VEGETABLE SKEWERS

Preparation Time	Total Time	Yield
10 minutes	55 minutes	6 servings

INGREDIENTS

- 1/4 cup (60 ml) olive oil
- 1/4 cup (60 ml) lemon juice
- 1/4 teaspoon (0.5 g) dried parsley
- 1 (16 oz. or 450 g) package extra-firm tofu, cut into 1-inch pieces
- 1 medium (200 g) zucchini, cut into 1-inch pieces
- 2 medium white onion (about 120 g each), quartered
- 2 medium bell pepper (about 125 g each), cut into 1-inch pieces
- 1 cup (150 g) cherry tomatoes
- Salt and freshly ground black pepper
- 12 wooden skewers

METHOD

- Whisk together the oil, lemon juice, and parsley in a large bowl.
- Add the tofu, zucchini, onion, bell pepper, and cherry tomatoes. Toss to coat and season to taste. Let it sit for 30-40 minutes to absorb flavors.
- Preheat your grill or griddle to high.
- Thread the tofu and vegetables alternately onto the wooden skewers.
- Grill the tofu skewers for 15 minutes, turning once

halfway through cooking time.
- Transfer to a serving dish.
- Enjoy.

NUTRITIONAL INFORMATION

Energy	Fat	Carbohydrates	Protein	Sodium
165 calories	11.9 g	10.2 g	7.7 g	215 mg

TOFU AND VEGETABLE STIR-FRY

Preparation Time	Total Time	Yield
10 minutes	25 minutes	4 servings

INGREDIENTS

- 3 tablespoons (45 ml) olive oil
- 1 (16 oz. or 450 g) package extra-firm tofu
- 1 medium (120 g) onion, chopped
- 2 cloves (6 g) garlic, minced
- 2 cups (240 g) broccoli florets, cut into small pieces
- 1 medium (125 g) red bell pepper, cut into 1-inch pieces
- 3 oz. (85 g) snap peas, trimmed
- Salt and freshly ground black pepper

METHOD

- Cut the tofu into 1-inch slices
- Heat 2 tablespoons of oil in a non-stick pan or skillet over medium-high flame. Fry the tofu slices until golden brown. Transfer to a chopping board and cut into 1-inch cubes. Set aside.
- Heat the remaining 1 tablespoon olive oil in the same pan. Stir-fry onion and garlic for about 3 minutes.
- Next, add the broccoli florets, bell pepper, and snap peas. Cook, stirring for 6-7 minutes.
- Add the tofu and season with salt and pepper; cook for another 3-5 minutes.
- Transfer to a serving dish.
- Serve and enjoy.

NUTRITIONAL INFORMATION

Energy	Fat	Carbohydrates	Protein	Sodium
224 calories	15.6 g	13.3 g	12.3 g	322 mg

THAI CURRIED TOFU

Preparation Time	Total Time	Yield
10 minutes	35 minutes	4 servings

INGREDIENTS

- 2 tablespoons (30 ml) vegetable oil
- 1 medium (125 g) red onion, thinly sliced
- 2 cloves (6 g) garlic, minced
- 1 tablespoon (10 g) fresh ginger, thinly sliced
- 1 ½ tablespoons (10 g) red curry powder
- 1/2 teaspoon (1 g) cayenne pepper
- 1/4 teaspoon (0.5 g) ground cloves
- 1 cup (250 g) coconut cream
- 1 cup (250 ml) chicken stock
- 1 (16 oz. or 450 g) package extra-firm tofu, cut into small cubes
- 1/4 cup (15 g) fresh coriander leaves, chopped
- Salt and freshly ground black pepper

METHOD

- Heat oil in a medium saucepan over medium-high flame. Stir-fry onion, garlic, and ginger for 3-4 minutes.
- Add the curry powder, cayenne pepper, and ground cloves. Cook for 1 minute, stirring constantly.
- Next, stir in the stock and bring to a boil.
- Add the coconut cream, tofu, and coriander. Simmer for 10-15 minutes, stirring frequently but gently. Season with salt and pepper. Remove from heat.
- Transfer to a serving dish.
- Serve and enjoy.

NUTRITIONAL INFORMATION

Energy	Fat	Carbohydrates	Protein	Sodium
274 calories	22.9 g	11.0 g	11.5 g	318 mg

PAN-FRIED TOFU WITH MUSHROOM AND HERB

Preparation Time	Total Time	Yield
10 minutes	30 minutes	4 servings

INGREDIENTS

- 1 (16 oz. or 450 g) package extra-firm tofu
- 2 tablespoons (30 ml) olive oil
- 2 tablespoons (30 g) butter
- 3 cloves (10 g) garlic, minced
- 1 ½ cups (225 g) button mushrooms, thinly sliced
- 1 tablespoon (15 ml) Worcestershire sauce
- 2 tablespoons (30 ml) rice wine vinegar
- 1/2 cup (30 g) fresh chives, chopped

METHOD

- Cut the tofu into 1-inch slices.
- Heat the olive oil in a non-stick pan or skillet over medium-high flame. Fry the tofu slices until golden brown. Transfer them to a clean plate and set aside.
- Using the same pan, melt butter over medium flame. Stir-fry garlic for 1-2 minutes.
- Add the mushrooms, Worcestershire sauce, and rice wine vinegar. Cook for another 4-5 minutes, stirring often. Season with salt and pepper.
- Divide the tofu among 4 individual plates then top with sautéed mushrooms. Garnish with chopped chives.

- Serve and enjoy.

NUTRITIONAL INFORMATION

Energy	Fat	Carbohydrates	Protein	Sodium
250 calories	18.9 g	2.6 g	15.8 g	180 mg

SPICY ORANGE GLAZED SHRIMPS WITH TOFU

Preparation Time	Total Time	Yield
10 minutes	25 minutes	8 servings

INGREDIENTS

- 2 tablespoons (30 ml) vegetable oil
- 1 (16 oz. or 450 g) package extra-firm tofu
- 2 tablespoons (30 g) butter
- 1/3 cup (85 ml) orange juice concentrate
- 2 tablespoons (30 g) chili-garlic sauce
- 1 pound (450 g) medium shrimps, head removed
- 1/4 cup (15 g) scallions, chopped
- Salt and freshly ground black pepper

METHOD

- Cut the tofu into 1-inch slices.
- Heat the vegetable oil in a non-stick pan or skillet over medium-high flame. Fry tofu until golden brown. Then, transfer to a chopping board and cut into 1-inch cubes. Set aside.
- Melt butter in the same pan and then add the orange juice concentrate and chili-garlic sauce; cook for 30 seconds.
- Add the shrimps and tofu; cook for about 5-7 minutes, stirring to coat everything with spicy orange glaze. Season with salt and pepper. Remove from heat.
- Transfer to a serving dish and then sprinkle with scallions.

- Serve immediately and enjoy.

NUTRITIONAL INFORMATION

Energy	Fat	Carbohydrates	Protein	Sodium
206 calories	12.4 g	3.8 g	20.2 g	352 mg

SPICY MUSHROOM TOFU AND BOK-CHOY

Preparation Time	Total Time	Yield
10 minutes	25 minutes	6 servings

INGREDIENTS

- 2 tablespoons (30 ml) olive oil
- 1 (16 oz. or 450 g) package silken tofu, cut into small cubes
- 1 medium (120 g) onion, chopped
- 2 cloves (6 g) garlic, minced
- 2 cups (300 g) mushrooms, thinly sliced
- 1 cup (250 ml) chicken stock, unsalted
- 2 tablespoons (30 g) oyster sauce
- 2 teaspoons (10 g) chili paste
- 1 head bok-choy (about 300 g), leaves separated
- Salt and freshly ground black pepper

METHOD

- Heat olive oil in a skillet over medium-high flame. Stir-fry onion and garlic for about 3 minutes.
- Add the mushrooms, tofu, chicken stock, oyster sauce, and chili paste. Cook for 5 minutes, stirring frequently.
- Add the bok-choy leaves. Season with salt and pepper. Cook further 3 minutes, stirring occasionally.
- Transfer to a serving dish.
- Serve and enjoy.

NUTRITIONAL INFORMATION

Energy	Fat	Carbohydrates	Protein	Sodium
178 calories	11.6 g	8.6 g	13.6 g	206 mg

STIR-FRIED KALE WITH TOFU AND SESAME

Preparation Time	Total Time	Yield
10 minutes	20 minutes	6 servings

INGREDIENTS

- 3 tablespoons (45 ml) vegetable oil
- 1 (16 oz. or 450 g) package firm tofu, sliced about 1-inch thick
- 1 shallot (about 40 g), thinly sliced
- 2 cloves (6 g) garlic, minced
- 2.2 pounds (1 kg) Tuscan kale, torn and tough stems removed
- 2 tablespoons (20 g) sesame seeds, toasted
- 1 teaspoon (5 ml) sesame oil
- Salt and freshly ground black pepper

METHOD

- Heat 2 tablespoons of oil in a non-stick pan or skillet over medium-high flame. Fry tofu until golden brown. Transfer to a chopping board and then cut into 1-inch cubes. Set aside.
- Heat the remaining 1 tablespoon oil using the same pan. Stir-fry shallot and garlic for about 3 minutes.
- Add the kale; cook, stirring for 2-3 minutes.
- Add the tofu and season with salt and pepper. Cook for another-3 minutes. Remove from heat and then stir in sesame oil.
- Transfer to a serving dish and sprinkle with sesame

seeds.
- Serve and enjoy.

NUTRITIONAL INFORMATION

Energy	Fat	Carbohydrates	Protein	Sodium
214 calories	12.2 g	19.4 g	12.2 g	264 mg

THAI TOFU CURRY

Preparation Time	Total Time	Yield
10 minutes	30 minutes	6 servings

INGREDIENTS

- 2 tablespoons (30 ml) vegetable oil
- 1 medium (125 g) red onion, thinly sliced
- 2 cloves (6 g) garlic, minced
- 1 ½ tablespoons (10 g) curry powder
- 1/2 teaspoon (1 g) turmeric powder
- 1/4 teaspoon (0.5 g) ground cloves
- 1 (14 oz. or 400 g) can of coconut milk
- 1 cup (250 ml) vegetable stock, unsalted
- 1 (16 oz. or 450 g) package silken tofu, cut into 1-inch cubes
- 1/4 cup (15 g) fresh cilantro
- 1 (10 g) red hot chili pepper
- 2 tablespoons (30 ml) fish sauce
- Salt and freshly ground black pepper

METHOD

- Heat oil in a medium saucepan over medium-high flame. Stir-fry onion, garlic, and ginger for 3-4 minutes.
- Add the curry powder, turmeric, and cloves. Cook for 1 minute, stirring constantly.
- Stir in the vegetable stock and bring to a boil.
- Add the coconut milk, tofu, cilantro, chili pepper, and fish sauce. Simmer for 10-15 minutes, stirring frequently but gently. Season with salt and pepper. Remove from heat.
- Transfer to a serving dish.

- Serve and enjoy.

NUTRITIONAL INFORMATION

Energy	Fat	Carbohydrates	Protein	Sodium
257 calories	22.2 g	8.9 g	7.5 g	396 mg

TOFU AND BOK-CHOY STIR-FRY

Preparation Time	Total Time	Yield
10 minutes	20 minutes	4 servings

INGREDIENTS

- 3 tablespoons (45 ml) olive oil
- 1 (16 oz. or 450 g) package firm tofu, cubed, about 1-inch
- 1/2 cup shallots, chopped
- 2 cloves (6 g) garlic, minced
- 1 head bok-choy, leaves separated
- 2 tablespoons (30 g) oyster sauce
- 1 teaspoon (5 ml) Worcestershire sauce
- Salt and freshly ground black pepper

METHOD

- In a non-stick fry pan or skillet, heat 2 tablespoons of oil over medium-high flame. Fry the tofu until golden brown. Transfer to a cutting board and then cut into 1-inch cubes. Set aside.
- Heat the remaining oil using the same pan. Stir-fry shallots and garlic for about 2 minutes.
- Add the bok-choy, tofu, oyster sauce, and Worcestershire sauce; cook, stirring for 5 minutes. Season with salt and pepper. Remove from heat.
- Transfer to a serving dish.
- Serve and enjoy.

NUTRITIONAL INFORMATION

Energy	Fat	Carbohydrates	Protein	Sodium
205 calories	15.2 g	8.9 g	11.2 g	292 mg

TOFU WITH CHILI-GARLIC SAUCE

Preparation Time	Total Time	Yield
10 minutes	25 minutes	6 servings

INGREDIENTS

- 2 tablespoons (30 ml) soybean oil
- 1 medium (120 g) onion, chopped
- 1 tablespoon (10 g) garlic, minced
- 1 teaspoon (5 g) ginger, ground
- 2 tablespoons (30 g) chili-garlic sauce
- 1 cup (250 ml) chicken stock, unsalted
- 1/4 cup (60 ml) reduced-sodium soy sauce
- 2 teaspoons (10 g) brown sugar
- 2.2 pounds (1 kg g) silken tofu, cut into 1 inch pieces
- 1 teaspoon (5 ml) sesame oil
- 1/4 cup (15 g) spring onions, chopped
- Salt and freshly ground black pepper

METHOD

- Heat the soybean oil in a skillet over medium-high flame. Stir-fry onion and garlic for about 3-4 minutes.
- Add the ginger powder and chili-garlic sauce. Cook, stirring for about 1 minute.
- Add the chicken stock, soy sauce, and brown sugar. Bring to a boil.
- Add the tofu. Cook, stirring gently for 3-5 minutes. Remove from heat. Stir in sesame oil and season with salt and pepper.

- Transfer to a serving dish. Sprinkle with spring onions.
- Serve and enjoy.

NUTRITIONAL INFORMATION

Energy	Fat	Carbohydrates	Protein	Sodium
173 calories	10.0 g	8.7 g	12.6 g	544 mg

MIXED VEGGIE AND TOFU STIR-FRY

Preparation Time	Total Time	Yield
10 minutes	25 minutes	4 servings

INGREDIENTS

- 3 tablespoons (45 ml) olive oil
- 1 (16 oz. or 450 g) package firm tofu
- 1 medium (120 g) red onion, sliced
- 2 cloves (6 g) garlic, minced
- 2 cups (240 g) broccoli florets, cut into small pieces
- 1 cup (150 g) button mushroom, sliced
- 1 medium (200 g) zucchini, thinly sliced
- 1 medium (120 g) red bell pepper, cut into 1-inch pieces
- 1/2 cup (85 g) frozen green peas (thawed)
- Salt and freshly ground black pepper

METHOD

- Cut the tofu into 1-inch slices.
- Heat 2 tablespoons of oil in a non-stick pan and skillet over medium-high flame. Fry the tofu until golden brown. Transfer to a clean plate. Cut into 1-inch cubes. Set aside.
- Heat the remaining 1 tablespoon oil in the same pan. Sauté onion and garlic until aromatic, about 3 minutes.
- Add the broccoli florets, mushrooms, zucchini, bell pepper, and green peas. Cook, stirring for 5 minutes.
- Add the tofu and season with salt and pepper to taste. Cook further 2-3 minutes.

- Transfer to a serving dish.
- Serve and enjoy.

NUTRITIONAL INFORMATION

Energy	Fat	Carbohydrates	Protein	Sodium
224 calories	14.0 g	15.9 g	11.9 g	212 mg

ROASTED VEGGIES WITH TOFU

Preparation Time	Total Time	Yield
10 minutes	35 minutes	4 servings

INGREDIENTS

- 1/4 cup (60 ml) olive oil
- 1/4 cup (60 ml) balsamic vinegar
- 1/4 teaspoon (0.5 g) dried oregano
- 1 (16 oz. or 450 g) package extra-firm tofu, cut into small cubes
- 1 head broccoli (about 300 g), cut into small florets
- 8 oz. (250 g) green beans, trimmed and cut into 2-inch pieces
- 1 cup (170 g) green peas
- Salt and freshly ground black pepper

METHOD

- Preheat and set your oven to 425 F (210 C).
- Whisk together the oil, balsamic vinegar, and oregano in a large bowl.
- Add the tofu, broccoli, green beans, and green peas. Toss to coat and season to taste. Transfer to a baking dish.
- Bake the tofu and vegetables in the oven for 25 minutes.
- Serve and enjoy.

NUTRITIONAL INFORMATION

Energy	Fat	Carbohydrates	Protein	Sodium
263 calories	17.8 g	16.4 g	14.3 g	219 mg

TOFU WITH GARLIC AND SWEET CHILI SAUCE

Preparation Time	Total Time	Yield
10 minutes	20 minutes	4 servings

INGREDIENTS

- 2 tablespoons (30 g) butter
- 1 teaspoon (3 g) garlic, minced
- 1/2 cup (125 g) sweet-chili sauce
- 2 tablespoons (30 ml) rice wine vinegar
- 1 (16 oz. or 450 g) package firm tofu, fried
- Steamed vegetables, to serve

METHOD

- Cut the fried tofu into small cubes and then set aside.
- Melt the butter in a non-stick pan or skillet over medium-high flame. Stir-fry garlic until fragrant, about 1-2 minutes.
- Add the sweet-chili sauce and rice wine vinegar; cook for 1 minute, stirring constantly.
- Next, add the tofu and toss to coat; cook further 3 to 5 minutes.
- Serve in a platter along with steamed vegetables.
- Enjoy.

NUTRITIONAL INFORMATION

Energy	Fat	Carbohydrates	Protein	Sodium
192 calories	10.5 g	16.6 g	9.3 g	233 mg

VEGETARIAN TOFU BURGER

Preparation Time	Total Time	Yield
15 minutes	45 minutes	6 servings

INGREDIENTS

- 1 (16 oz. or 450 g) package silken tofu, crumbled
- 1 cup (100 g) breadcrumbs
- 1 medium egg (about 50 g)
- 1 large onion (150 g), chopped
- 1/4 cup (15 g) fresh coriander, chopped
- 2 tablespoons (30 ml) soy sauce
- 1 tablespoon (15 g) Worcestershire sauce
- Salt and freshly ground black pepper

METHOD

- Mix together the tofu, breadcrumbs, egg, onion, coriander, soy sauce, and Worcestershire sauce in a medium mixing bowl. Season with salt and pepper. Cover and place in the chiller for 30 minutes.
- Preheat your griddle or grill to medium high.
- Take about 1/4 cup of tofu mixture and form into a patty. Repeat with the remaining mixture.
- Grill your tofu burgers for 5-7 minutes on each side or until golden brown and grill marks form.
- Serve on hamburger bun with veggies and your choice of dressing.
- Enjoy.

NUTRITIONAL INFORMATION

Energy	Fat	Carbohydrates	Protein	Sodium
144 calories	3.7 g	18.1 g	9.1 g	395 mg

WATER SPINACH TOFU AND GINGER STIR-FRY

Preparation Time	Total Time	Yield
10 minutes	20 minutes	4 servings

INGREDIENTS

- 3 tablespoons (45 ml) olive oil
- 1 (16 oz. or 450 g) package firm tofu, cut into 1-inch slices
- 1 medium (120 g) onion, chopped
- 2 cloves (6 g) garlic, minced
- 1 teaspoon (5 g) fresh ginger, grated
- 1 pound (450 g) water spinach, washed, picked and tough stems removed
- 2 tablespoons (30 g) oyster sauce
- 2 teaspoon (10 g) Worcestershire sauce
- Salt and freshly ground black pepper

METHOD

- In a non-stick pan or skillet, heat 2 tablespoons oil over medium-high flame. Fry the tofu until golden brown. Transfer to a chopping board and then cut into thin strips. Set aside.
- Heat the remaining 1 tablespoon of oil using the same pan. Stir-fry onion and garlic for 2-3 minutes.
- Add the water spinach, tofu, oyster sauce, and Worcestershire sauce. Cook for 5 minutes, stirring often. Season with salt and pepper. Remove from heat.
- Transfer to a serving dish.
- Serve and enjoy.

NUTRITIONAL INFORMATION

Energy	Fat	Carbohydrates	Protein	Sodium
208 calories	15.5 g	9.5 g	12.6 g	372 mg

TOFU AND STRAW MUSHROOM IN OYSTER SAUCE

Preparation Time	Total Time	Yield
5 minutes	20 minutes	4 servings

INGREDIENTS

- 3 tablespoons (45 ml) olive oil
- 1 (16 oz. or 450 g) package firm tofu, cut into 1-inch slices
- 1 medium (120 g) onion chopped
- 2 cloves (6 g) garlic, minced
- 1 cup (180 g) straw mushrooms
- 2 tablespoons (30 g) mirin
- 2 tablespoons (30 ml) soy sauce
- Salt and freshly ground black pepper

METHOD

- In a non-stick pan or skillet, heat 2 tablespoons oil over medium-high heat. Fry tofu until golden brown. Transfer to a chopping board and then cut into small pieces. Set aside.
- Heat the remaining 1 tablespoon of oil in the same pan. Add the onion and garlic; stir-fry for 3-4 minutes.
- Add the straw mushrooms; cook for 3-5 minutes.
- Add the tofu, mirin, and soy sauce; cook further 3 minutes, stirring often. Season with salt and pepper. Remove from heat.
- Transfer to a serving dish.

- Serve and enjoy.

NUTRITIONAL INFORMATION

Energy	Fat	Carbohydrates	Protein	Sodium
213 calories	15.5 g	11.2 g	11.9 g	607 mg

TOFU IN CREAM OF MUSHROOM SAUCE

Preparation Time	Total Time	Yield
10 minutes	30 minutes	6 servings

INGREDIENTS

- 1 (16 oz. or 450 g) package firm tofu
- 1/2 cup (60 g) flour
- 2 tablespoons (30 ml) vegetable oil
- 1 tablespoon (15 g) butter, unsalted
- 1 teaspoon (3 g) garlic, minced
- 1 (10.75 ounce) can condensed cream of mushroom soup
- 2 cups (300 g) button mushrooms, sliced
- 1/2 cup (125 ml) water
- 1 medium (60 g) carrot, diced
- 1 cup (250 ml) milk
- 2 tablespoons (30 ml) soy sauce
- 1/2 teaspoon (1 g) dried parsley
- Salt and freshly ground black pepper

METHOD

- Cut the fried tofu into small cubes. Dredge with flour and then set aside.
- Heat oil in a non-stick pan over medium-high flame. Fry the tofu until golden brown. Place them in a clean plate and set aside.
- Melt butter using the same pan over medium flame. Stir-fry garlic for 1-2 minutes
- Add the cream of mushroom soup, water, mushrooms,

and carrot. Simmer for about 8-10 minutes, stirring often.
- Next, stir in the milk, soy sauce, and parsley. Then, add the tofu cook further 3 to 5 minutes. Season with salt and pepper.
- Transfer to a serving dish.
- Serve and enjoy.

NUTRITIONAL INFORMATION

Energy	Fat	Carbohydrates	Protein	Sodium
208 calories	12.1 g	16.1 g	11.0 g	611 mg

BITTER MELON AND TOFU SAUTE

Preparation Time	Total Time	Yield
10 minutes	25 minutes	4 servings

INGREDIENTS

- 2 tablespoons (30 ml) olive oil
- 1 (16 oz. or 450 g) package firm tofu, cut into small cubes
- 2 shallots (about 40 g), chopped
- 2 cloves (6 g) garlic, minced
- 1 medium (125 g) tomato, thinly sliced
- 1 medium (200 g) bitter melon
- 1 large egg (about 60 g), beaten
- Salt and freshly ground black pepper

METHOD

- Slice the bitter melon lengthwise. Using a spoon, scoop out the white part with the seeds. Thinly slice the green part crosswise.
- Heat 2 tablespoon of oil in a non-stick pan or skillet over medium-high flame. Add the shallots and garlic; stir –fry for 2-3 minutes.
- Add the chopped tomato and cook for another 2-3 minutes or until softened.
- Add the bitter melon. Cook, stirring for 5-7 minutes.
- Stir in the beaten egg. Cook for another 3-5 minutes, stirring frequently. Season with salt and pepper.
- Serve and enjoy.

NUTRITIONAL INFORMATION

Energy	Fat	Carbohydrates	Protein	Sodium
186 calories	13.0 g	8.8 g	12.0 g	281 mg

ORANGE GLAZED GRILLED TOFU

Preparation Time	Total Time	Yield
10 minutes	20 minutes	8 servings

INGREDIENTS

- 1 (16 oz. or 450 g) package firm tofu
- 1/2 cup (125 ml) orange juice concentrate
- 2 tablespoons (30 ml) soy sauce
- 1/4 teaspoon (0.5 g) paprika
- 1/4 teaspoon (0.5 g) cumin (ground)
- 3 tablespoons (45 g) butter
- Freshly ground black pepper

METHOD

- Cut the tofu to make ½-inch thick slices.
- Combine the orange juice concentrate, soy sauce, and paprika in a non-reactive container. Add the tofu slices and turn to coat all sides. Season with pepper to taste. Cover and place in the fridge for at least an hour.
- Melt 2 tablespoons of butter in a non-stick fry pan over medium flame. Cook the tofu slices until golden brown. Transfer to a serving dish. Cover with foil to keep warm.
- Using the same pan, melt the remaining butter over medium heat. Add the marinade and cook for 5 minutes to make a glaze.
- Drizzle the tofu slices with orange glaze.

- Serve and enjoy.

NUTRITIONAL INFORMATION

Energy	Fat	Carbohydrates	Protein	Sodium
174 calories	13.4 g	5.8 g	10.1 g	426 mg

CUMIN SPICED TOFU SCRAMBLE

Preparation Time	Total Time	Yield
5 minutes	15 minutes	4 servings

INGREDIENTS

- 2 tablespoons (30 g) butter
- 1 medium (120 g) white onion, chopped
- 1 teaspoon (3 g) garlic, minced
- 2 medium tomatoes (about 125 g each), chopped
- 1 (16 oz. or 450 g) package firm tofu, crumbled
- 1/2 teaspoon (1 g) cumin, ground
- Salt and freshly ground black pepper
- Fresh basil, for garnish

METHOD

- Melt butter in a skillet over medium-high flame. Stir-fry onion and garlic until fragrant.
- Add the tomatoes. Cook for about 3-4 minutes, stirring often until softened.
- Add the tofu and cumin. Cook, stirring for 3-5 minutes more and then season with salt and pepper.
- Transfer to a serving dish and garnish with fresh basil.
- Serve and enjoy.

NUTRITIONAL INFORMATION

Energy	Fat	Carbohydrates	Protein	Sodium
154 calories	10.7 g	7.2 g	10.3 g	264 mg

TOFU BURGER PATTIES WITH CHEDDAR

Preparation Time	Total Time	Yield
10 minutes	50 minutes	6 servings

INGREDIENTS

- 1 (16 oz.) package silken tofu, crumbled
- 1 cup (100 g) breadcrumbs
- 1 medium (50 g) egg
- 1 large onion (about 60 g), chopped
- 1 medium (60 g) carrot, chopped
- 1 celery stalk (60 g), chopped
- 1/2 cup (60 g) cheddar cheese, grated
- 1/4 cup (15 g) fresh cilantro, chopped
- 1 tablespoon (15 ml) Worcestershire sauce
- Salt and freshly ground black pepper

METHOD

- Combine the tofu, breadcrumbs, egg, onion, carrot, celery, cheddar cheese, cilantro, and Worcestershire sauce in a large mixing bowl. Season with salt and pepper. Cover and place in the chiller for 30 minutes.
- Preheat your griddle or grill to medium high.
- Take about ¼ cup of mixture and form into a burger patty. Repeat with the remaining mixture.
- Grill your tofu burgers for 5–7 minutes on each side or until golden brown and grill marks form.
- Serve on hamburger bun with veggies and your choice of dressing.

- Enjoy.

NUTRITIONAL INFORMATION

Energy	Fat	Carbohydrates	Protein	Sodium
184 calories	6.9 g	18.9 g	11.3 g	363 mg

CHOW MEIN WITH TOFU

Preparation Time	Total Time	Yield
10 minutes	25 minutes	4 servings

INGREDIENTS

- 2 tablespoons (30 ml) peanut oil
- 1 (16 oz. or 450 g) package firm tofu, diced
- 1 medium (120 g) brown onion, finely chopped
- 2 cloves (6 g) garlic, crushed
- 1 large carrot (about 100 g), peeled, finely chopped
- 8 button mushrooms, thinly sliced
- 1 celery stalk (about 60 g), cut into strips
- 1 cup (250 ml) chicken stock, unsalted
- 1/4 cup (60 g) oyster sauce
- 2 tablespoons (30 ml) reduced-sodium soy sauce
- 1 (10 oz. or 300 g) package fresh egg noodles
- 1/2 cup (85 g) frozen peas, thawed
- 1/2 cup (30 g) spring onions, chopped
- Freshly ground black pepper

METHOD

- Heat the peanut oil in a wok or skillet over high flame.
- Add the onion and garlic; stir-fry for 2-3 minutes.
- Add the carrot, mushrooms, and celery; stir-fry for about 3 minutes or until vegetables are crisp-tender.
- Add the chicken stock, oyster sauce, soy sauce, and fresh egg noodles. Cook, stirring often for 3-5 minutes or until the mixture boils and thickens slightly.

- Add the tofu, peas, and spring onion. Cook for another 3-5 minutes. Toss to mix well and season with pepper to taste.
- Divide evenly among individual bowls.
- Enjoy.

NUTRITIONAL INFORMATION

Energy	Fat	Carbohydrates	Protein	Sodium
298 calories	13.4 g	31.5 g	16.3 g	621 mg

EASY TOFU BURGER

Preparation Time	Total Time	Yield
10 minutes	15 minutes	2 servings

INGREDIENTS

- 1 tablespoon (15 ml) olive oil
- 2 tofu burger patties (about 125 g each)
- 2 hamburger buns, split
- 2 round slices onion
- 2 round slices tomato
- 2 slices cheddar cheese (2 ounces each)
- 4 lettuce leaves
- Choice of dressing, to serve

METHOD

- Heat oil in a medium non-stick fry pan over medium-high heat. Cook burger patties until golden brown.
- Heat burger buns in a toaster oven.
- Fill each hamburger bun with lettuce, tomato, tofu burger, cheese, and onion. Serve with your choice of dressing.
- Enjoy.

NUTRITIONAL INFORMATION

Energy	Fat	Carbohydrates	Protein	Sodium
341 calories	23.5 g	18.5 g	16.9 g	344 mg

OPEN FACED SANDWICH WITH TOFU SALAD

Preparation Time	Total Time	Yield
15 minutes	15 minutes	4 servings

INGREDIENTS

- 1/4 cup (60 ml) olive oil
- 1/4 cup (60 ml) lemon juice
- 1 tablespoon (20 ml) honey
- 1 tablespoon (15 g) Dijon mustard
- 3 oz. or 85 g iceberg lettuce, shredded
- 8 oz. or 250 g firm tofu, diced
- 1 cup (150 g) cherry tomatoes, quartered
- 2 oz. or 60 g black olives, sliced
- 1/4 cup (15 g) flat-leaf parsley, chopped
- 4 large slices wholegrain bread
- Salt and freshly ground black pepper

METHOD

- In a medium bowl, whisk together the olive oil, lemon juice, honey, and Dijon mustard.
- Add the lettuce, tofu, olives, cherry tomatoes, and parsley. Toss to coat with dressing and then season with salt and pepper.
- Divide the tofu salad mixture among bread slices.
- Serve immediately and enjoy.

NUTRITIONAL INFORMATION

Energy	Fat	Carbohydrates	Protein	Sodium
269 calories	17.9 g	21.1 g	9.0 g	390 mg

CUCUMBER AND TOFU SALAD WITH SCALLIONS

Preparation Time	Total Time	Yield
15 minutes	15 minutes	6 servings

INGREDIENTS

- 2 medium cucumbers (about 200 g each), diced
- 1 (16 oz. or 450 g) package silken tofu, steamed and diced
- 3/4 cup (45 g) scallions, chopped
- Salt and freshly ground black pepper

Dressing:

- 1/4 cup (60 ml) rice wine vinegar
- 1/4 cup (60 ml) olive oil
- 1 tablespoon (20 ml) honey
- 1 teaspoon (15 ml) lime juice

METHOD

- In a medium bowl, whisk together the rice wine vinegar, olive oil, honey, and lime juice.
- Add the cucumbers, tofu, and scallions. Toss to coat with dressing and then season with salt and pepper.
- Divide among 6 individual bowls.
- Serve immediately and enjoy.

NUTRITIONAL INFORMATION

Energy	Fat	Carbohydrates	Protein	Sodium
150 calories	10.5 g	8.0 g	5.9 g	227 mg

GARDEN FRESH SALAD WITH TOFU

Preparation Time	Total Time	Yield
10 minutes	10 minutes	6 servings

INGREDIENTS

- 2 cups (300 g) grape tomatoes
- 1 medium (200 g) cucumber, diced
- 1 (16 oz. and 450 g) package silken tofu, steamed and cubed
- 1 medium (125 g) yellow bell pepper, thinly sliced
- 1 head Romaine lettuce (about 350 g), torn into small pieces
- 1/4 cup (30 g) grated parmesan cheese
- Salt and freshly ground black pepper

Red Wine Vinaigrette Dressing:

- 1/4 cup (60 ml) olive oil
- 1/4 cup (60 ml) red wine vinegar
- 1 tablespoon (20 ml) honey
- 2 teaspoons (10 g) Dijon mustard

METHOD

- In a small bowl, whisk together the olive oil, red wine vinegar, honey, and Dijon mustard. Set aside.
- In a large bowl, add the grape tomatoes, cucumber, tofu, bell pepper, and lettuce. Toss to combine all of the ingredients and season with salt and pepper.
- Divide among 6 individual bowls. Drizzle with prepared Red Wine Vinaigrette and sprinkle with parmesan.

- Serve and enjoy.

NUTRITIONAL INFORMATION

Energy	Fat	Carbohydrates	Protein	Sodium
185 calories	12.9 g	11.7 g	9.0 g	276 mg

QUINOA SALAD WITH TOFU

Preparation Time	Total Time	Yield
10 minutes	10 minutes	4 servings

INGREDIENTS

- 1/2 pound (225 g) steamed tofu, diced
- 2 cups (340 g) cooked quinoa
- 1 cup (150 g) cherry tomatoes, quartered
- 1 medium (200 g) cucumber, diced
- 1 celery stalk (about 60 g), diced
- 1/4 cup (15 g) scallions, chopped
- 2 tablespoons (7 g) fresh parsley, chopped
- Salt and freshly ground black pepper
- Baby spinach, to serve

Lemon Vinaigrette Dressing:

- 1/4 cup (60 ml) lemon juice
- 1/4 cup (60 ml) olive oil
- 1 tablespoon (20 ml) agave nectar
- 1 tablespoon (15 g) Dijon mustard

METHOD

- Combine all ingredients for the Lemon Vinaigrette in a salad bowl. Then, add the quinoa, tofu, cherry tomatoes, cucumber, celery, scallions, and parsley. Toss to coat with dressing and season with salt and pepper.
- Place a handful of spinach onto each serving dish

and then top with quinoa-tofu salad.

• Serve and enjoy.

NUTRITIONAL INFORMATION

Energy	Fat	Carbohydrates	Protein	Sodium
276 calories	15.1 g	31.3 g	6.7 g	229 mg

SPINACH SALAD WITH PAN-FRIED TOFU

Preparation Time	Total Time	Yield
15 minutes	15 minutes	4 servings

INGREDIENTS

- 1 (16 oz. or 450 g) package silken tofu, pan-fried
- 8 oz. (250 g) baby spinach
- 2 cups (300 g) cherry tomatoes (halved)
- 1 medium (200 g) cucumber (thinly sliced)
- Salt and freshly ground black pepper

Dressing:
- 1/4 cup (60 ml) lime juice
- 1/4 cup (60 ml) olive oil
- 1 tablespoon (20 ml) honey
- 1 tablespoon (15 g) Dijon mustard

METHOD

- Cut the pan-fried tofu into small cubes and then place in a large bowl.
- Add the spinach, cherry tomatoes, and cucumber. Toss to combine all of the ingredients and then season with salt and pepper.
- In a small bowl, mix together the lime juice, olive oil, honey, and Dijon mustard.
- Divide the salad among individual bowls. Drizzle with dressing.
- Serve and enjoy.

NUTRITIONAL INFORMATION

Energy	Fat	Carbohydrates	Protein	Sodium
231 calories	16.2 g	14.3 g	10.2 g	262 mg

RADISH SALAD WITH TOFU

Preparation Time	Total Time	Yield
15 minutes	15 minutes	4 servings

INGREDIENTS

- 4 medium radishes, thinly sliced
- 1 (16 oz. or 450 g) package silken tofu, steamed and cubed
- 1 head iceberg lettuce, torn
- 1/2 cup (30 g) chives, chopped
- Salt and freshly ground black pepper
- Fresh parsley (for garnish)

Dressing:

- 1/4 cup (85 ml) olive oil
- 1/4 cup (85 ml) balsamic vinegar
- 1 tablespoon (15 g) Dijon mustard
- 1 tablespoon (20 ml) honey

METHOD

- In a small bowl, whisk together the olive oil, balsamic vinegar, Dijon mustard, and honey. Set aside.
- Place the radishes, tofu, lettuce, and chives in a medium bowl. Toss to combine all of the ingredients and season to taste.
- Divide salad among 4 individual bowls. Drizzle with dressing. Garnish with fresh parsley.
- Serve immediately and enjoy.

NUTRITIONAL INFORMATION

Energy	Fat	Carbohydrates	Protein	Sodium
213 calories	16.0 g	10.1 g	8.5 g	239 mg

CRISPY TOFU BITES

Preparation Time	Total Time	Yield
10 minutes	30 minutes	6 servings

INGREDIENTS

- 1 ½ cups (150 g) bread crumbs
- 1 teaspoon (2 g) garlic powder
- 1/2 teaspoon (1 g) paprika
- 1/2 teaspoon (1 g) ground black pepper
- 2 (16 oz. or 450 g) package firm tofu, cut into small cubes
- 1 cup (125 g) flour
- 2 medium eggs (about 50 g each), beaten
- Vegetable oil, for frying
- Choice of dip, to serve

METHOD

- Combine the breadcrumbs, garlic powder, paprika, and pepper in a medium bowl. Set aside.
- Dredge tofu with flour. Next, dip in egg and then coat with seasoned breadcrumbs.
- Heat a generous amount of oil in a deep saucepan over medium-high flame. Deep fry tofu until golden brown. Then, place them in a plate lined with paper towels to drain excess oil.
- Transfer to a serving dish and serve with your choice of dip.
- Enjoy.

NUTRITIONAL INFORMATION

Energy	Fat	Carbohydrates	Protein	Sodium
220 calories	6.1 g	29.2 g	12.8 g	228 mg

FRIED TOFU WITH TOASTED GARLIC

Preparation Time	Total Time	Yield
10 minutes	20 minutes	4 servings

INGREDIENTS

- 3/4 cup (90 g) flour
- 1 teaspoon (3 g) garlic powder
- 1/2 teaspoon (2.5 g) salt
- 1/2 teaspoon (1 g) cumin, ground
- 1/2 teaspoon (1 g) ground black pepper
- 1 (16 oz. or 450 g) package firm tofu, cut into 1-inch thick slices
- 3/4 cup (185 ml) milk
- 1/4 cup (30 g) toasted garlic
- Vegetable oil, for frying

METHOD

- Combine flour, garlic, salt cumin, and pepper in a shallow bowl.
- Dip the tofu slices in milk and then place it in the flour mixture to coat.
- Heat a generous amount of oil in a deep saucepan over medium-high flame. Deep fry the tofu until golden brown. Then, place them in a plate lined with paper towels to drain excess oil.
- Place in a serving dish and top with toasted garlic.
- Serve and enjoy.

NUTRITIONAL INFORMATION

Energy	Fat	Carbohydrates	Protein	Sodium
202 calories	6.0 g	25.2 g	13.9 g	198 mg

CRISPY TOFU STICKS WITH SOY CHILI DIP

Preparation Time	Total Time	Yield
10 minutes	15 minutes	8 servings

INGREDIENTS

- 1 ½ cups (150 g) bread crumbs
- 1 teaspoon (2 g) onion powder
- 1/2 teaspoon (1 g) dried thyme
- 1/4 teaspoon (0.5 g) ground black pepper
- 2 (16 oz. or 450 g) package firm tofu
- 1 cup (125 g) flour
- 2 medium eggs (about 50 g each), beaten
- Vegetable oil, for frying

Dipping Sauce:

- 1/4 cup (60 ml) reduced-sodium soy sauce
- 2 tablespoons (30 ml) rice wine vinegar
- 1 (10 g) red hot chili pepper, chopped

METHOD

- Cut the tofu into 3-inch sticks.
- Combine the breadcrumbs, onion powder, thyme, and pepper in a shallow bowl. Set aside.
- Dredge tofu with flour. Next dip in egg and then coat with seasoned breadcrumbs.
- Heat a generous amount of oil in a deep saucepan over medium-high flame. Deep fry the tofu until golden brown. Then, place them in a plate lined with

paper towels to drain excess oil.

- Mix together dipping sauce ingredients in a small bowl.
- Serve tofu sticks with dipping sauce on the side.
- Enjoy.

NUTRITIONAL INFORMATION

Energy	Fat	Carbohydrates	Protein	Sodium
272 calories	13.8 g	23.2 g	14.6 g	343 mg

TOFU BITES WITH PEANUT SAUCE

Preparation Time	Total Time	Yield
5 minutes	15 minutes	4 servings

INGREDIENTS

- 2 tablespoons (30 ml) peanut oil
- 1 (16 oz.) package extra-firm tofu

Peanut Sauce:

- 2 tablespoons (30 g) peanut butter
- 1 tablespoon (15 ml) soy sauce
- 1 tablespoon (15 ml) rice wine vinegar
- 1/4 teaspoon (1.5 g) fresh ginger, grated
- 1 clove (3 g) garlic, minced
- 1 tablespoon (10 g) dry roasted peanuts, coarsely chopped

METHOD

- Mix together peanut butter, soy sauce, vinegar, ginger, and garlic in a small bowl. Sprinkle with chopped peanuts.
- Cut the tofu into 1-inch slices.
- Heat the peanut oil in a non-stick pan or skillet over medium-high flame. Fry the tofu until golden brown. Transfer to a chopping board and cut into 1-inch cubes.
- Arrange the tofu bites in a platter with peanut sauce placed at the center.

- Serve and enjoy.

NUTRITIONAL INFORMATION

Energy	Fat	Carbohydrates	Protein	Sodium
205 calories	16.6 g	4.5 g	12.2 g	276 mg

TOFU AND LEEK SOUP WITH SESAME

Preparation Time	Total Time	Yield
10 minutes	20 minutes	4 servings

INGREDIENTS

- 2 tablespoons (30 ml) olive oil
- 4 oz. (125 g) leeks, chopped
- 1 teaspoon (3 g) garlic, minced
- 2 cups (250 ml) reduced sodium chicken stock
- 2 cups (250 ml) water
- 1 (16 oz. or 450 g) package firm tofu
- 1 teaspoon (5 ml) sesame oil
- Salt and freshly ground black pepper

METHOD

- Heat olive oil in a medium saucepan over medium flame. Stir-fry leeks for 1-2 minutes.
- Add the chicken stock and water. Bring to a boil.
- Add the tofu and cook for 5-7 minutes, stirring occasionally. Remove from heat.
- Stir in sesame oil and season with salt and pepper.
- Ladle in individual bowls.
- Serve and enjoy.

NUTRITIONAL INFORMATION

Energy	Fat	Carbohydrates	Protein	Sodium
167 calories	12.9 g	6.1 g	9.7 g	310 mg

TOFU AND SEAWEED SOUP WITH SESAME

Preparation Time	Total Time	Yield
10 minutes	20 minutes	4 servings

INGREDIENTS

- 2 tablespoons (30 ml) soybean oil
- 2 shallots (about 40 g each, chopped
- 1 clove (3 g) garlic, minced
- 2 cups (500 ml) vegetable stock
- 2 cups (500 ml) water
- 1 (16 oz. or 450 g) package firm tofu
- 1 cup (250 g) fresh seaweeds, cut into small pieces
- 1 tablespoon (10 g) sesame seeds, toasted
- 1 teaspoon (5 ml) sesame oil
- Salt and freshly ground black pepper

METHOD

- Heat the oil in a medium saucepan over medium-high flame. Stir-fry shallots and garlic for 1-2 minutes.
- Add the vegetable stock and water. Bring to a boil.
- Add the tofu and cook for 5-7 minutes, stirring occasionally. Remove from heat.
- Add the seaweeds and sesame oil. Season with salt and pepper to taste. Stir to combine.
- Ladle in individual bowls. Sprinkle with toasted sesame seeds.
- Serve and enjoy.

NUTRITIONAL INFORMATION

Energy	Fat	Carbohydrates	Protein	Sodium
240 calories	17.9 g	8.0 g	12.3 g	432 mg

MISO SOUP WITH SHRIMP AND TOFU

Preparation Time	Total Time	Yield
10 minutes	25 minutes	4 servings

INGREDIENTS

- 2 tablespoons (30 ml) soybean oil
- 1/2 cup (30 g) scallions, thinly sliced
- 1 clove (3 g) garlic, minced
- 2 tablespoons (30 g) miso paste
- 1 tablespoon (15 g) tamarind paste
- 2 cups (500 ml) vegetable stock
- 2 cups (500 ml) water
- 1 (16 oz. or 450 g) package firm tofu, cubed
- 6 oz. (180 g) fresh medium shrimps, peeled and deveined
- Salt and freshly ground black pepper

METHOD

- Heat the oil in a medium saucepan over medium-high flame. Then, stir-fry scallions and garlic for 1-2 minutes.
- Add the miso paste and tamarind paste. Cook, stirring for 1 minute.
- Add the vegetable stock and water. Bring to a boil.
- Add the tofu and cook for 5 minutes, stirring occasionally.
- Add the shrimps and cook for another 3-5 minutes. Season with salt and pepper.
- Ladle in individual bowls.

- Serve and enjoy.

NUTRITIONAL INFORMATION

Energy	Fat	Carbohydrates	Protein	Sodium
207 calories	12.6 g	6.5 g	19.7 g	617 mg

TOFU AND SHRIMP SOUP WITH CHIVES

Preparation Time	Total Time	Yield
10 minutes	30 minutes	4 servings

INGREDIENTS

- 2 tablespoons soybean oil
- 2 shallots (about 40 g each), chopped
- 1 clove (3 g) garlic, minced
- 2 cups (500 ml) reduced-sodium chicken stock
- 2 cups (500 ml) water
- 1 (16 oz. or 450 g) package firm tofu
- 6 oz. (180 g) fresh medium shrimps, peeled and deveined
- 1/4 cup (60 ml) lemon juice
- 1/4 cup (60 g) fresh chives, chopped
- 2 tablespoons (20 g) toasted garlic
- Salt and freshly ground black pepper

METHOD

- Heat the oil in a medium saucepan over medium-high flame. Add the shallots and garlic; stir-fry for 2-3 minutes.
- Add the chicken stock and water. Bring to a boil.
- Add the tofu and cook for 5-7 minutes, stirring occasionally.
- Add the shrimps and cook for another 3-5 minutes. Remove from heat.
- Add in the lemon juice and then season with salt and pepper.

- Ladle in individual bowls and sprinkle with chives and toasted garlic.
- Serve and enjoy.

NUTRITIONAL INFORMATION

Energy	Fat	Carbohydrates	Protein	Sodium
198 calories	12.1 g	5.8 g	19.1 g	405 mg

CHICKEN AND TOFU SOUP WITH CHIVES

Preparation Time	Total Time	Yield
10 minutes	30 minutes	6 servings

INGREDIENTS

- 2 tablespoons (30 ml) olive oil
- 1 medium (120 g) onion, thinly sliced
- 2 cloves garlic (6 g), minced
- 8 oz. (250 g) chicken breast fillet, cut into thin strips
- 2 cups (500 ml) chicken stock, reduced-sodium
- 2 cups (500 ml) water
- 1 (16 oz. or 450 ml) package silken tofu, cut into small cubes
- 1/4 cup (15 g) fresh chives, chopped
- Salt and freshly ground black pepper

METHOD

- Heat the oil in a medium saucepan over medium-high flame. Stir-fry onion and garlic until fragrant. Add the chicken and cook for 7-8 minutes, stirring often.
- Add the chicken stock and water. Let it boil and then lower the heat to medium. Simmer for about 10 minutes.
- Add the tofu and chives, and cook for another 3-4 minutes. Season with salt and pepper.
- Ladle in individual bowls.
- Serve and enjoy.

NUTRITIONAL INFORMATION

Energy	Fat	Carbohydrates	Protein	Sodium
168 calories	9.6 g	3.9 g	16.5 g	254 mg

SPICY MISO SOUP WITH TOFU

Preparation Time	Total Time	Yield
10 minutes	25 minutes	4 servings

INGREDIENTS

- 2 tablespoons (30 ml) soybean oil
- 1 medium (120 g) onion, thinly sliced
- 2 cloves (6 g) garlic, minced
- 2 tablespoons (30 g) miso paste
- 4 cups (1 L) water
- 1 (16 oz. or 450 g) package silken tofu
- 2 tablespoons (7 g) fresh coriander leaves, chopped
- 2 oz. (60 g) leek, thinly sliced
- 1 (10 g) red hot pepper, thinly sliced
- Salt and freshly ground black pepper

METHOD

- Heat the oil in a medium saucepan over medium-high flame. Stir-fry onion and garlic until fragrant.
- Add the miso paste and cook for 2-3 minutes, stirring often.
- Add 1 L of water and bring to a boil.
- Add the tofu, coriander, leek, and hot pepper. Cook for another 5-7 minutes. Season with salt and pepper.
- Ladle in individual bowls.
- Serve and enjoy.

NUTRITIONAL INFORMATION

Energy	Fat	Carbohydrates	Protein	Sodium
179 calories	10.7 g	12.2 g	9.8 g	368 mg

MANDARIN ORANGE ALMOND TOFU DESSERT

Preparation Time	Total Time	Yield
10 minutes	1 hour 30 minutes	6 servings

INGREDIENTS

- 8 oz. (250 g) silken tofu, cut into small cubes
- 1 cup (250 ml) soy milk, unsweetened
- 3 g agar strips
- 1/2 cup (100 g) sugar
- 1 cup (250 ml) water
- 2 cups (300 g) canned Mandarin oranges in light syrup

METHOD

- Combine the tofu and soy milk in a blender and process until smooth.
- Soak the agar strips with water in a small bowl for 10 minutes. Drain and transfer the agar strips to a medium saucepan. Add sugar and 1 cup of water; heat until dissolved completely.
- Stir in the blended tofu mixture and bring to a simmer over medium flame for 5 minutes.
- Pour into a large container. Tap to remove bubbles floating on top. Let cool and then chill for at least an hour or until set.
- Cut into cubes. Place in a medium glass bowl. Then, add the Mandarin oranges with light syrup. Stir to

combine.

- Ladle in individual dessert bowls.
- Serve and enjoy.

NUTRITIONAL INFORMATION

Energy	Fat	Carbohydrates	Protein	Sodium
213 calories	3.5 g	41.7 g	7.4 g	44 mg

MANGO AND ALMOND TOFU DESSERT

Preparation Time	Total Time	Yield
10 minutes	1 hour 20 minutes	4 servings

INGREDIENTS

- 2/3 cup (165 ml) boiling water
- 1 oz. (28 g) gelatin
- 8 oz. (250 g) firm silken tofu
- 1/2 cup (160 ml) honey
- 2 cups (500 ml) soy milk, unsweetened
- 1 teaspoon (5 ml) almond extract
- Fresh mint leaves, for garnish

Mango Compote:

- 2/3 cup (165 ml) water
- 1/4 cup (50 g) granulated sugar
- 1 ½ cups (240 g) mango, cut into small cubes
- 2 tablespoons (30 ml) lime juice

METHOD

- Whisk together boiling water and gelatin in a small bowl until the gelatin is completely dissolved.
- Cut the tofu into small cubes and place them in a food processor. Then, add the honey and soy milk. Process until smooth.
- Transfer the tofu mixture into a large bowl. Stir in gelatin mixture and almond extract. Mix gently to combine without making much bubbles.

- Ladle the mixture into 4 individual molds or ramekins. Place in the chiller for at least 1 hour or until set.
- Meanwhile, make the mango compote by bringing water and sugar to a boil. Then, add the mango cubes and lime juice. Cook for about 2 minutes. Turn off the heat and let it cool.
- Once the pudding is set, run a knife around the edges to loosen it up. Turn it over onto a plate to release the pudding.
- Top with mango compote and garnish with fresh mint leaves.
- Serve and enjoy.

NUTRITIONAL INFORMATION

Energy	Fat	Carbohydrates	Protein	Sodium
285 calories	4.0 g	54.3 g	11.6 g	95 mg

CHOCO TOFU PUDDING WITH RASPBERRIES

Preparation Time	Total Time	Yield
10 minutes	10 minutes	4 servings

INGREDIENTS

- 1 (1 lb. or 450 g) silken tofu
- 3/4 cup (185 ml) almond milk, unsweetened
- 1/3 cup (35 g) cocoa powder, unsweetened
- 1/3 cup (65 g) coconut sugar
- 2 teaspoons (10 ml) vanilla extract
- 1 cup (125 g) raspberries
- Fresh mint sprigs, for garnish

METHOD

- Combine the tofu, almond milk, cocoa powder, coconut sugar, and vanilla extract in a blender. Process until smooth.
- Divide among 4 dessert cups. Cover and place in the chiller until ready to serve.
- Top with raspberries and garnish with mint sprigs.
- Serve and enjoy.

NUTRITIONAL INFORMATION

Energy	Fat	Carbohydrates	Protein	Sodium
173 calories	4.8 g	28.4 g	8.0 g	41 mg

BANANA TOFU AND MATCHA PUDDING

Preparation Time	Total Time	Yield
10 minutes	10 minutes	4 servings

INGREDIENTS

- 16 oz. (450 g) silken tofu
- 1 large (150 g) banana, sliced
- 2/3 cup (165 ml) soy milk, unsweetened
- 3 tablespoons (15 g) Matcha powder
- 2 tablespoons (40 ml) honey
- 1 teaspoon (5 ml) vanilla extract
- 2 tablespoons (15 g) shredded coconut, to serve
- Fresh mint leaves, to serve

METHOD

- Add the tofu, banana, soy milk, matcha powder, honey, and vanilla extract in a blender or food processor. Process until smooth.
- Divide mixture among 4 dessert cups. Cover and place in the chiller until ready to serve.
- Sprinkle with shredded coconut and garnish with mint before serving.
- Enjoy.

NUTRITIONAL INFORMATION

Energy	Fat	Carbohydrates	Protein	Sodium
181 calories	4.7 g	22.2 g	11.2 g	63 mg

BERRY BANANA AND TOFU PUDDING

Preparation Time	Total Time	Yield
10 minutes	10 minutes	4 servings

INGREDIENTS

- 16 oz. (450 g) silken tofu
- 1 large (150 g) banana, sliced
- 2/3 cup (165 ml) soy milk, unsweetened
- 2 cups (440 g) frozen strawberries
- 1/4 cup (80 ml) maple syrup
- 1 teaspoon (5 ml) vanilla extract
- Fresh mint leaves, to serve

METHOD

- Add the tofu, banana, soy milk, strawberries, maple syrup, and vanilla extract in a blender or food processor. Process until smooth.
- Divide mixture among 4 dessert cups. Cover and place in the chiller until ready to serve.
- Garnish with mint before serving.
- Enjoy.

NUTRITIONAL INFORMATION

Energy	Fat	Carbohydrates	Protein	Sodium
200 calories	4.1 g	31.9 g	10.0 g	65 mg

RECIPE INDEX

Q

Quinoa Salad with Tofu 68

R

Radish Salad with Tofu 72
Roasted Veggies with Tofu 38

S

Spicy Miso Soup with Tofu 92
Spicy Mushroom Tofu and Bok-Choy 26
Spicy Orange Glazed Shrimps with Tofu 24
Spinach Salad with Pan-Fried Tofu 70
Stir-fried Kale with Tofu and Sesame 28

T

Thai Curried Tofu 20
Thai Tofu Curry 30
Tofu and Bok-Choy Stir-Fry 32
Tofu and Leek Soup with Sesame 82
Tofu and Seaweed Soup with Sesame 84
Tofu and Shrimp Soup with Chives 88
Tofu and Straw Mushroom in Oyster Sauce 46
Tofu and Vegetable Skewers 16
Tofu and Vegetable Stir-Fry 18
Tofu Bites with Peanut Sauce 80
Tofu Burger Patties with Cheddar 56
Tofu in Cream of Mushroom Sauce 48
Tofu Skewers with Sesame and Spicy Peanut Sauce 6
Tofu Veggie Kebabs 10
Tofu with Chili-Garlic Sauce 34
Tofu with Garlic and Sweet Chili Sauce 40
Tofu with Red Curry and Mixed Vegetables 12
Tofu with Sriracha Sauce 4
Traditional Ma Po Tofu 2

V

Vegetarian Tofu Burger 42

W

Water Spinach Tofu and Ginger Stir-Fry 44

Made in the USA
Las Vegas, NV
31 August 2022

54357725R00066